1

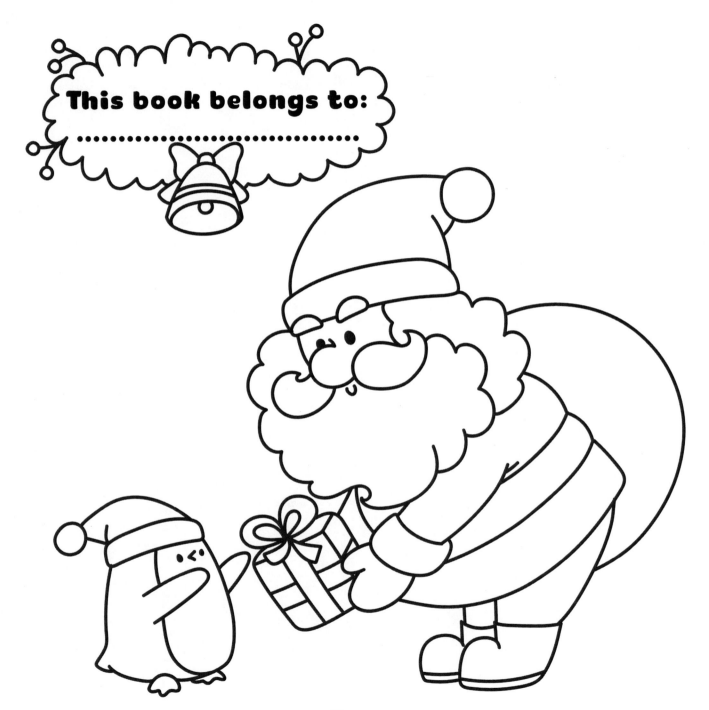

This book belongs to:
....

4

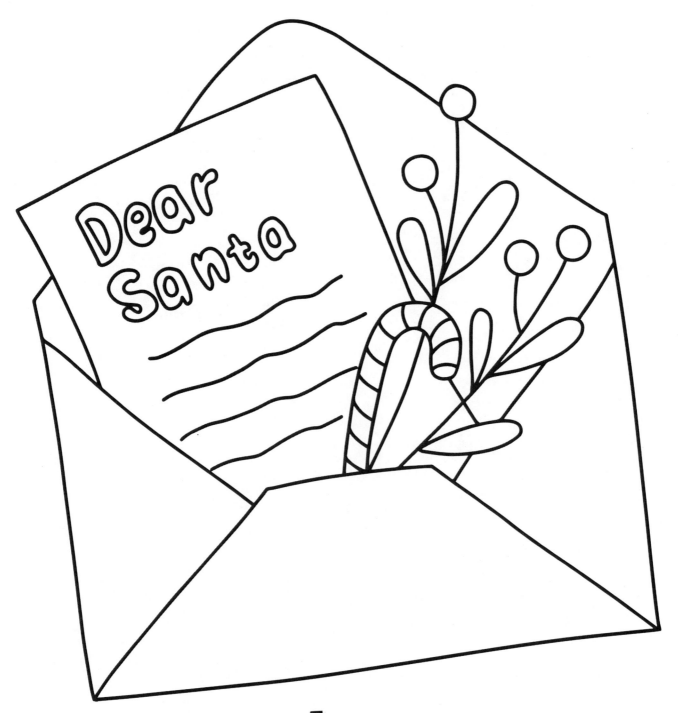

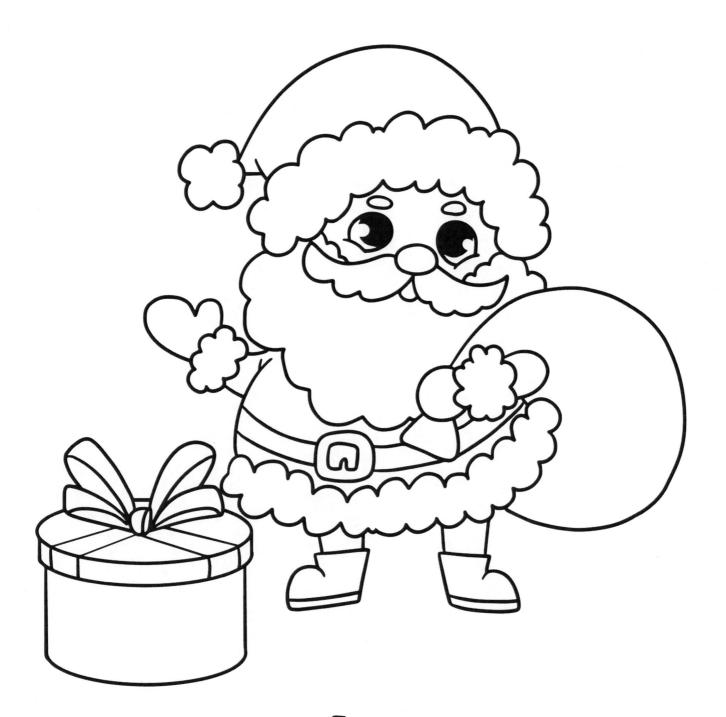

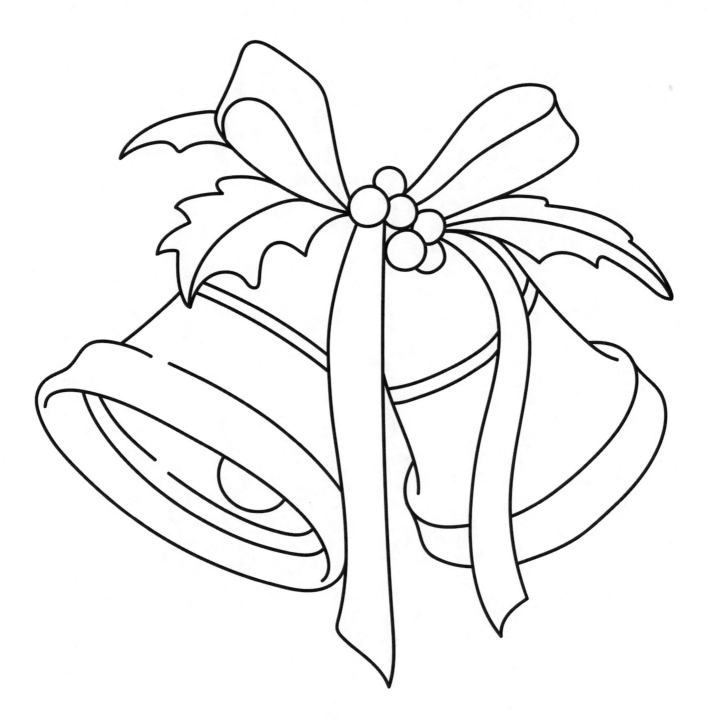

9

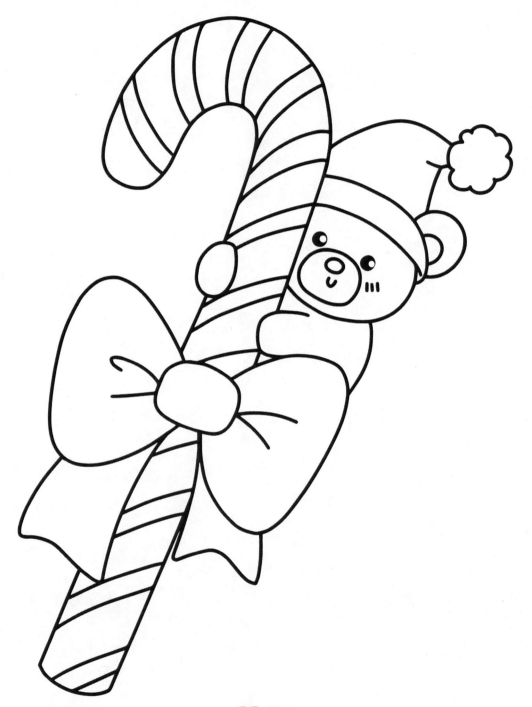

11

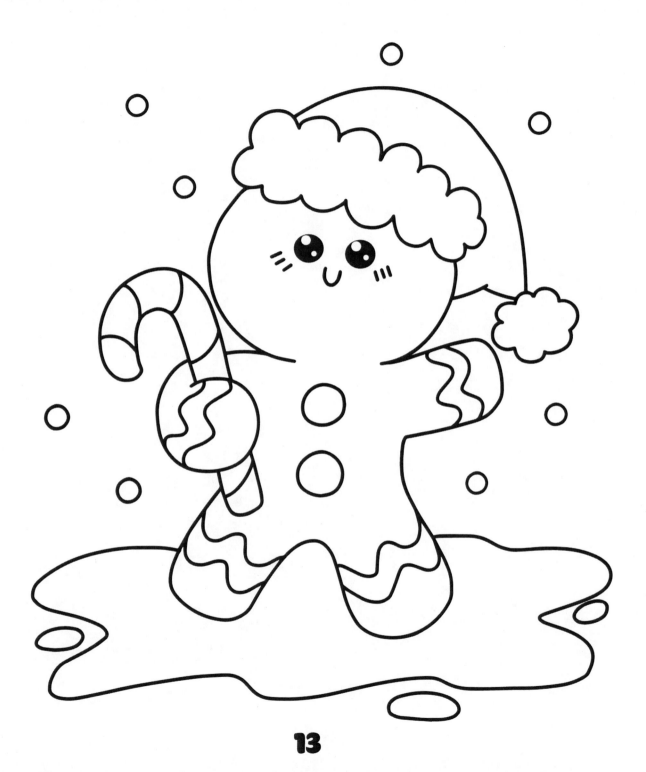

13

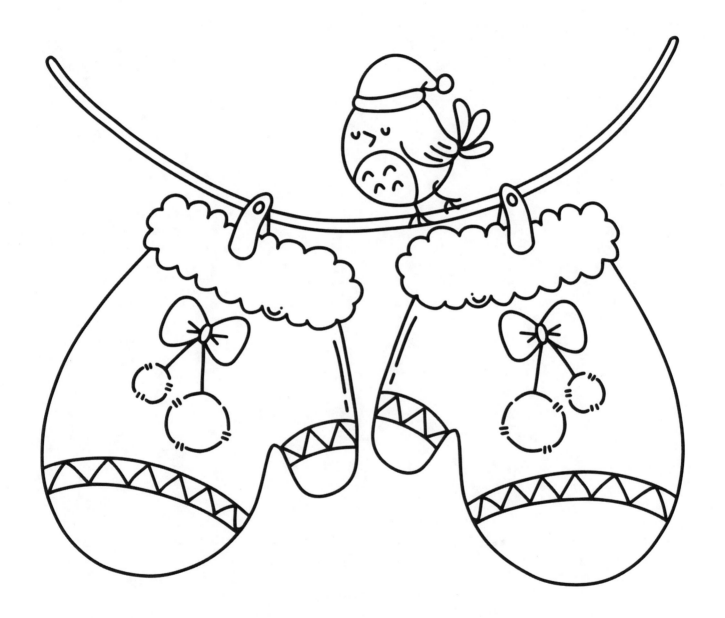

15

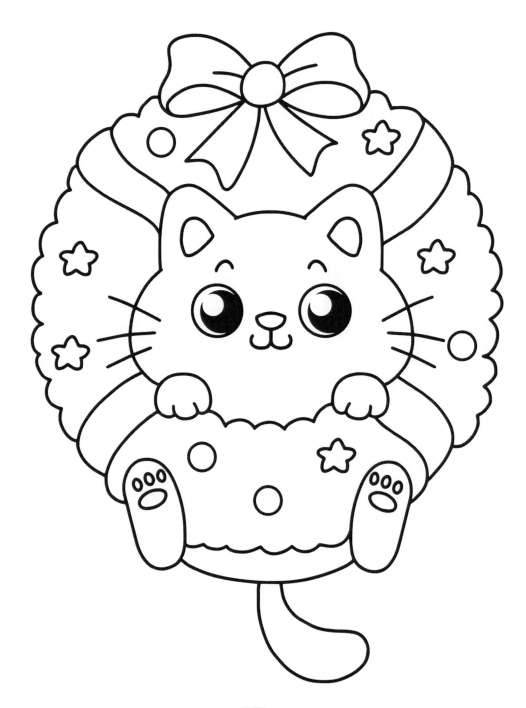

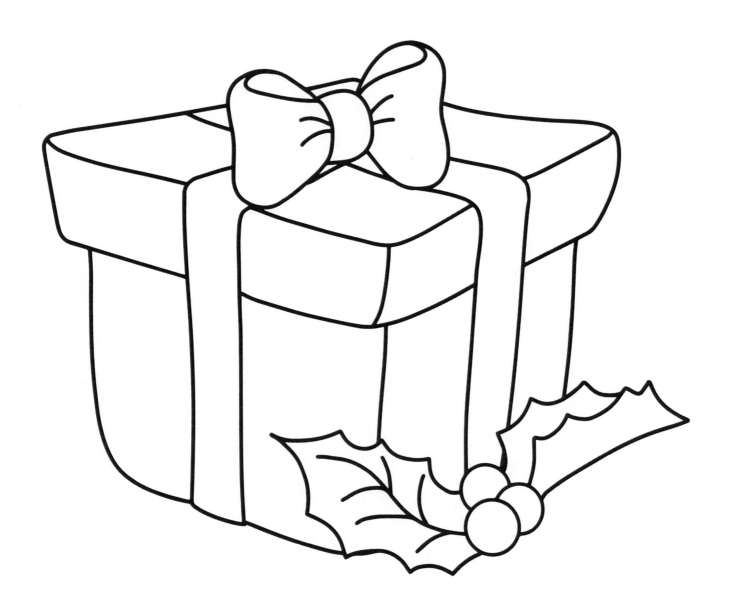

19

20

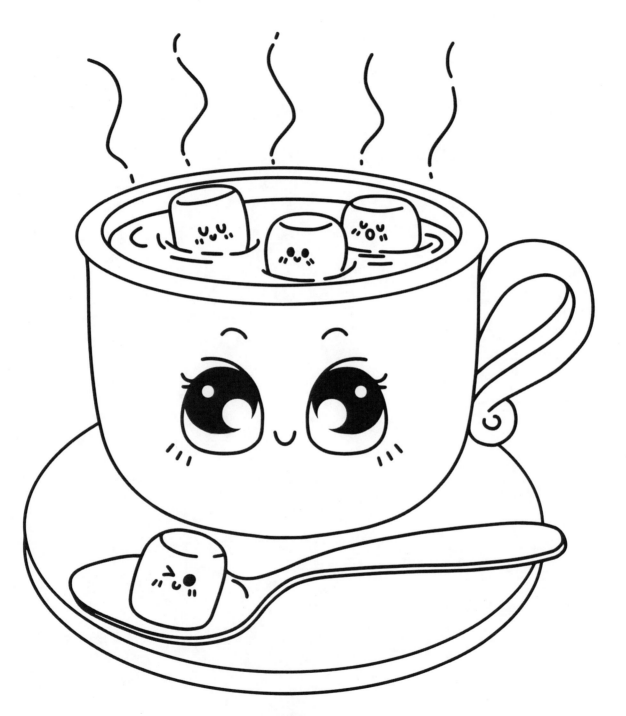

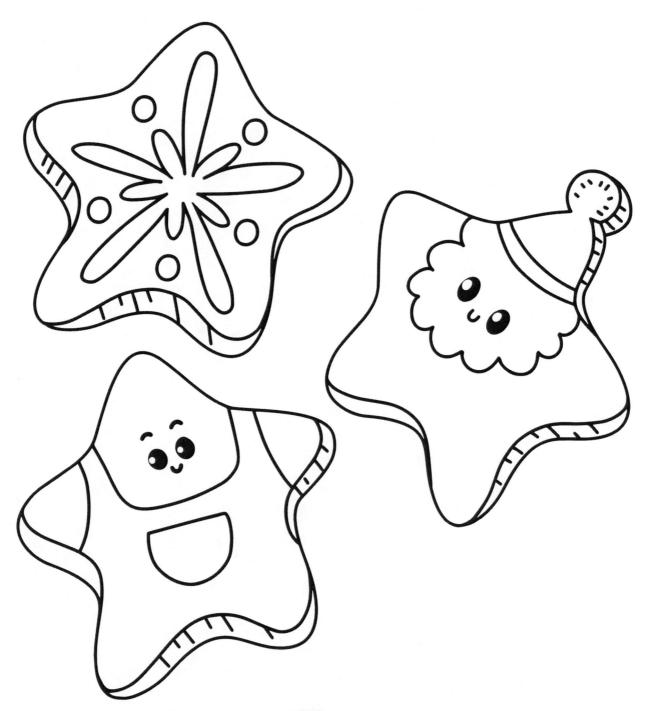

23

24

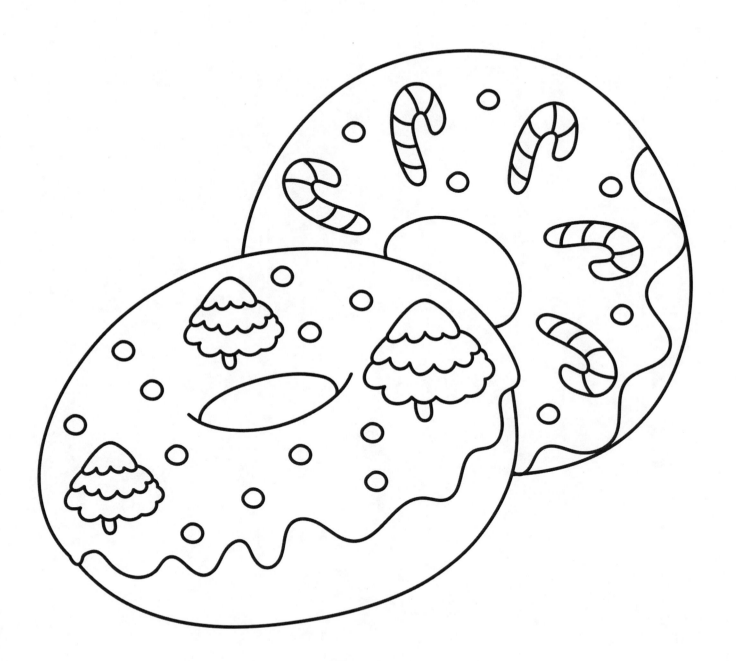

26

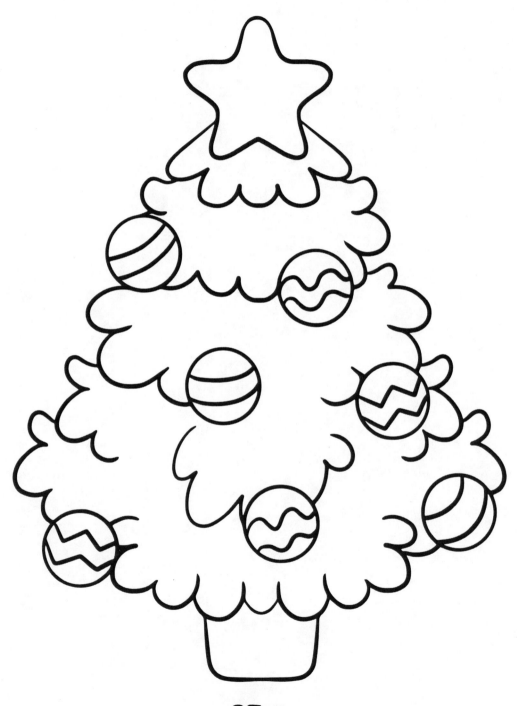

27

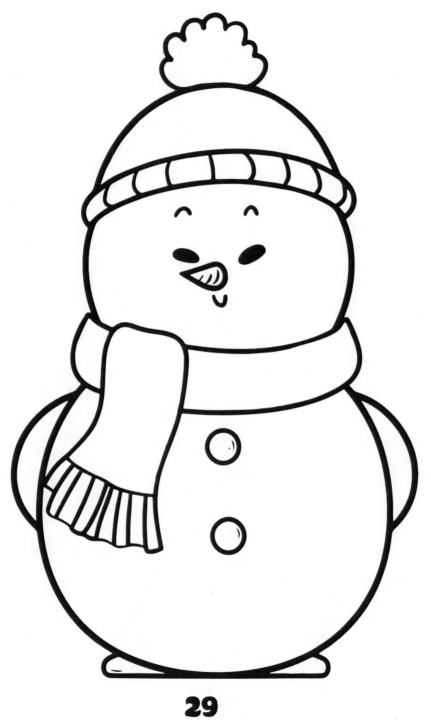

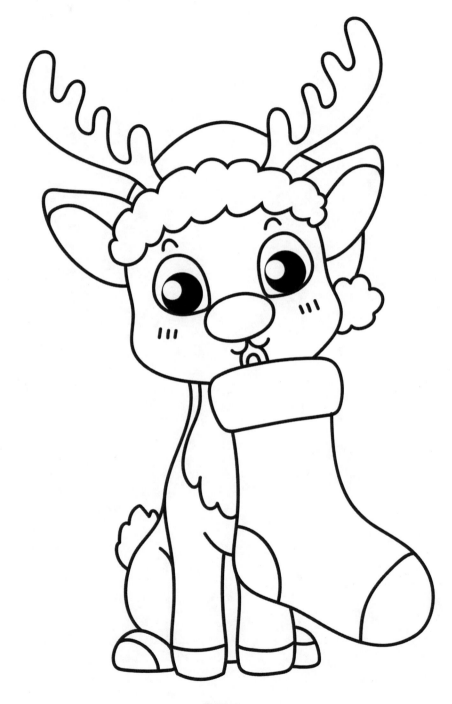

31

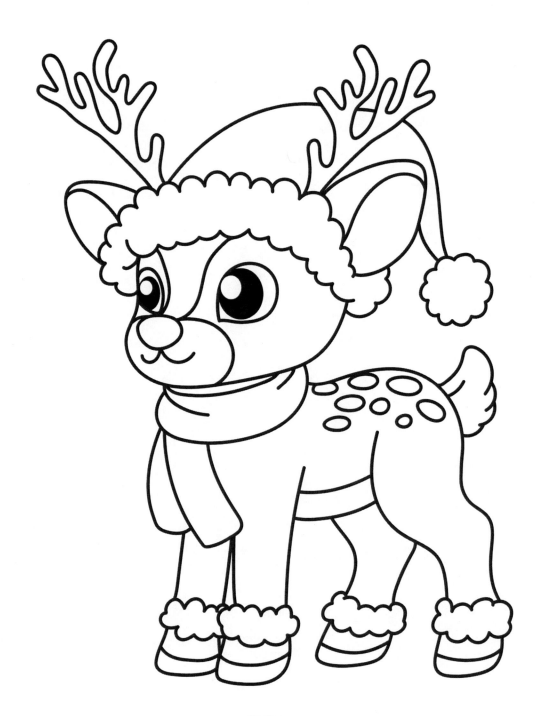

33

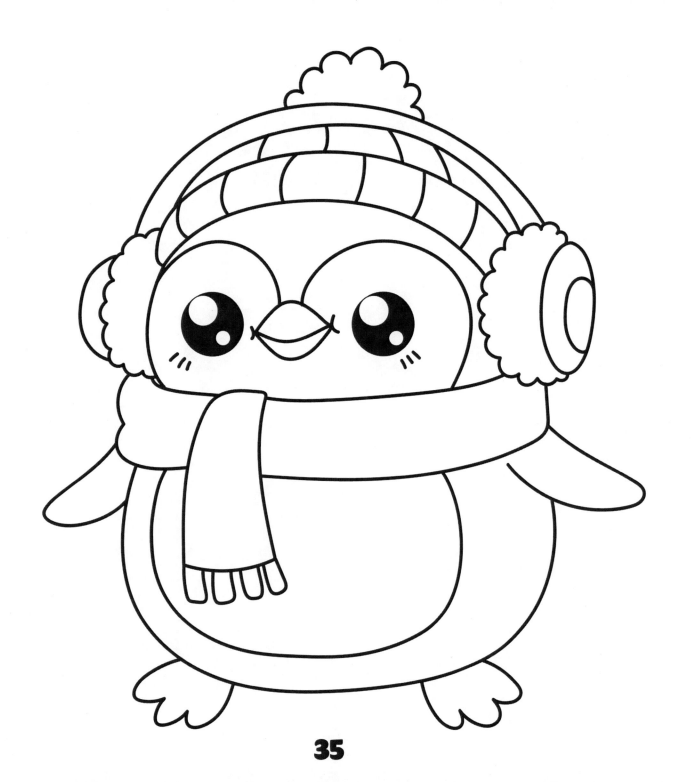

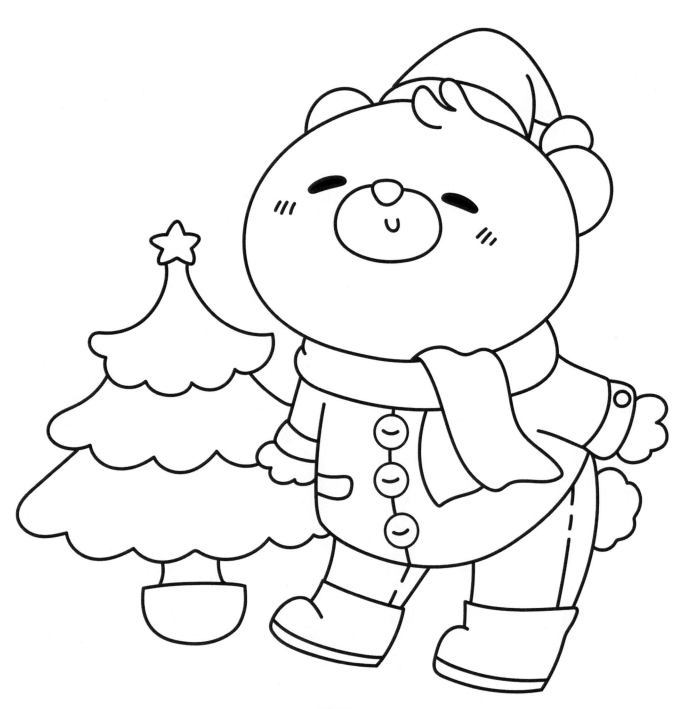

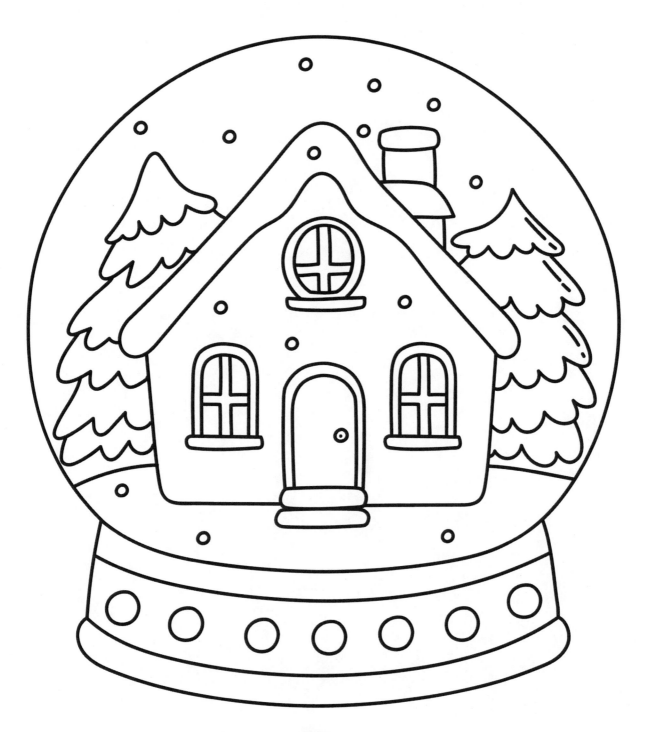

39

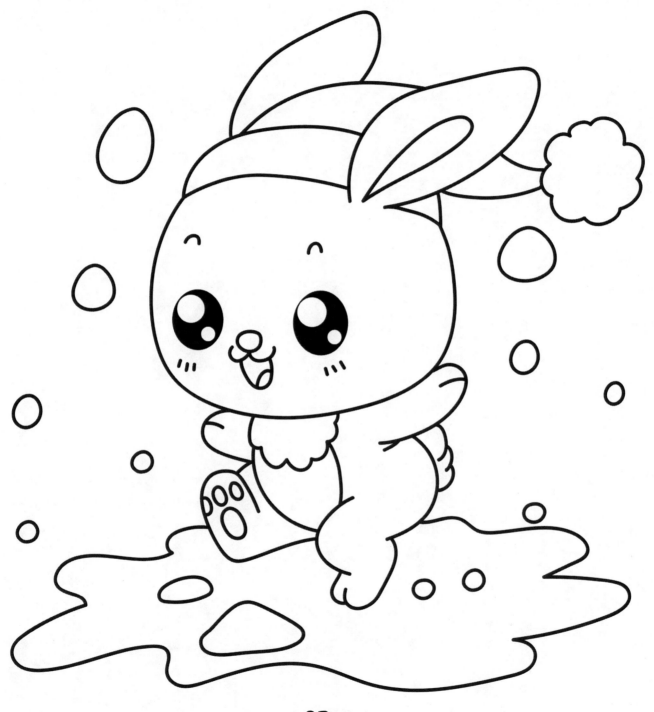

42

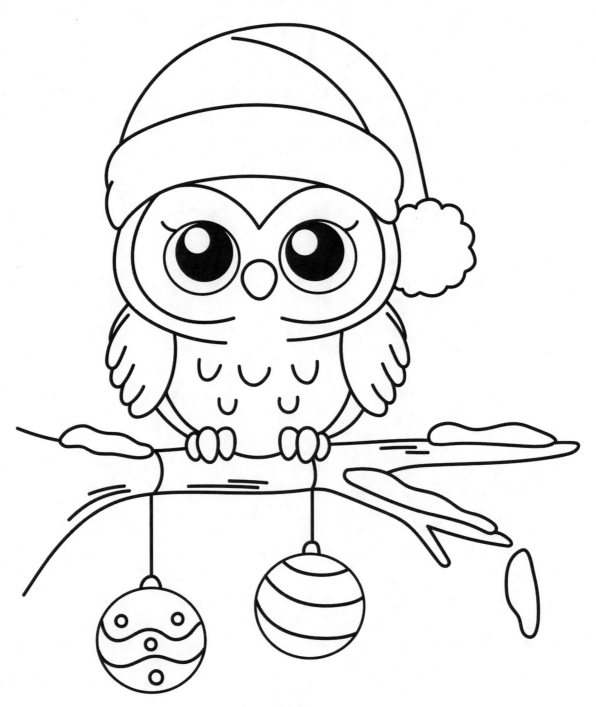

43

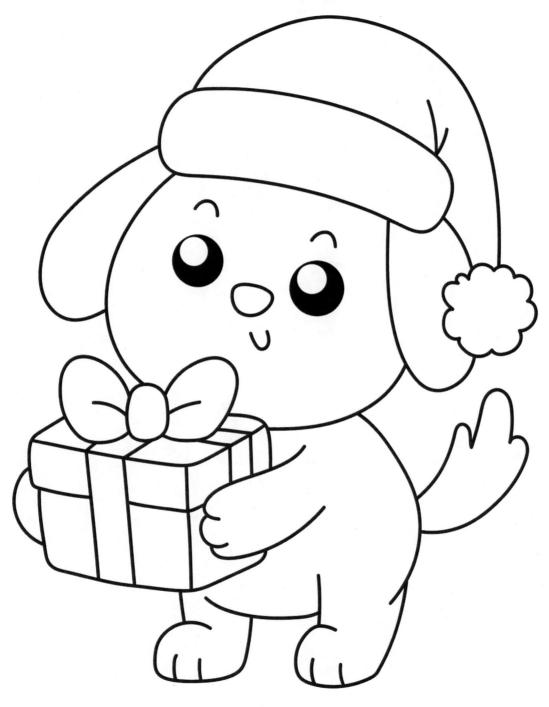

45

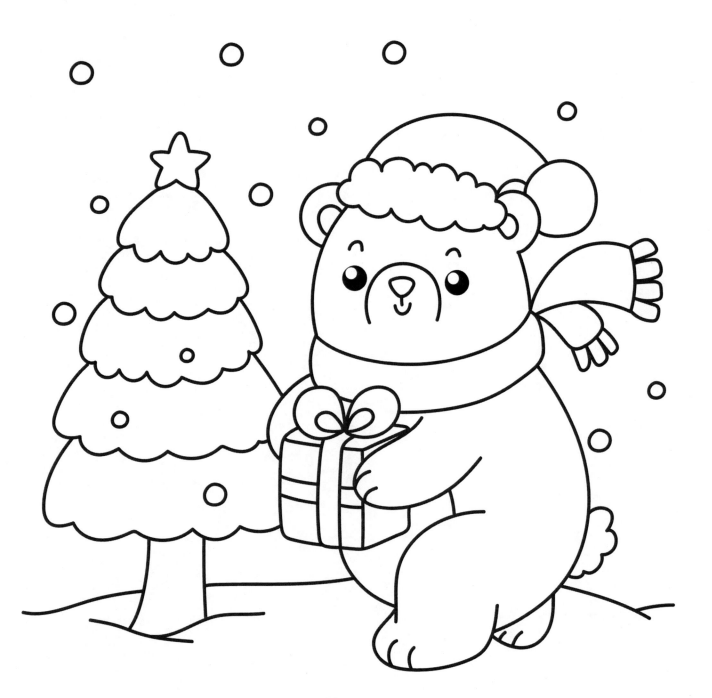

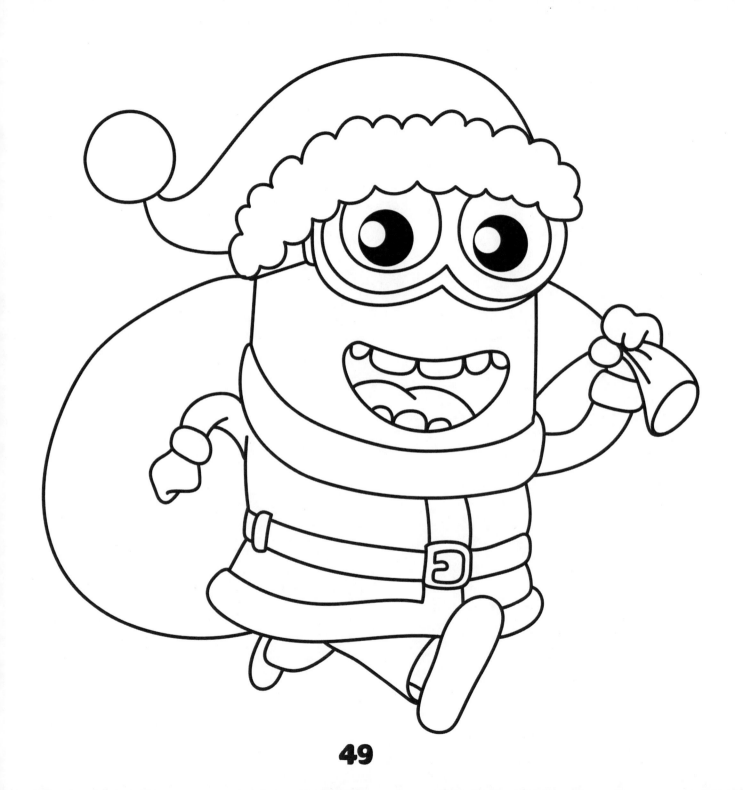

49

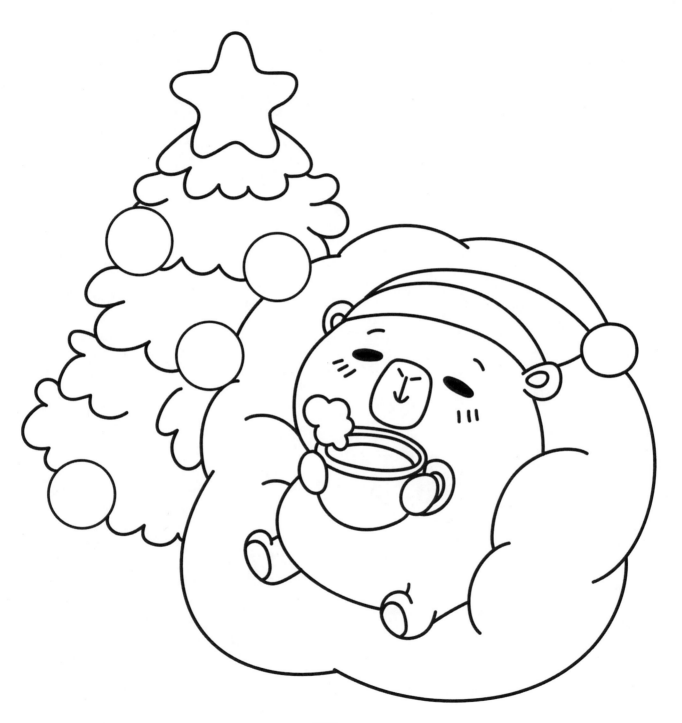

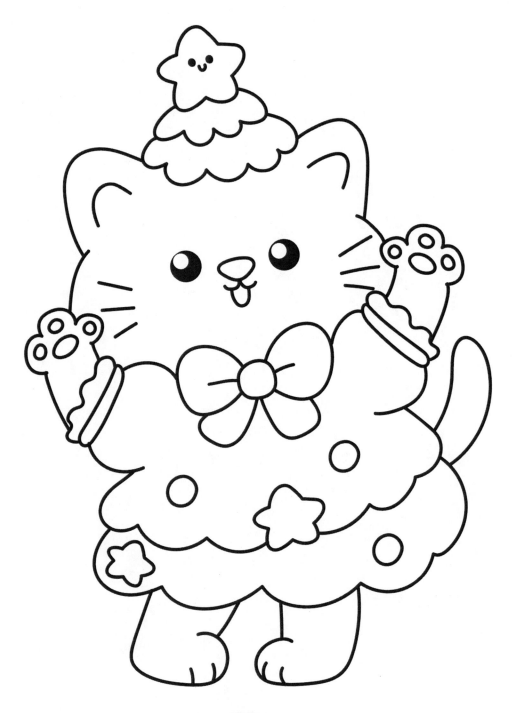

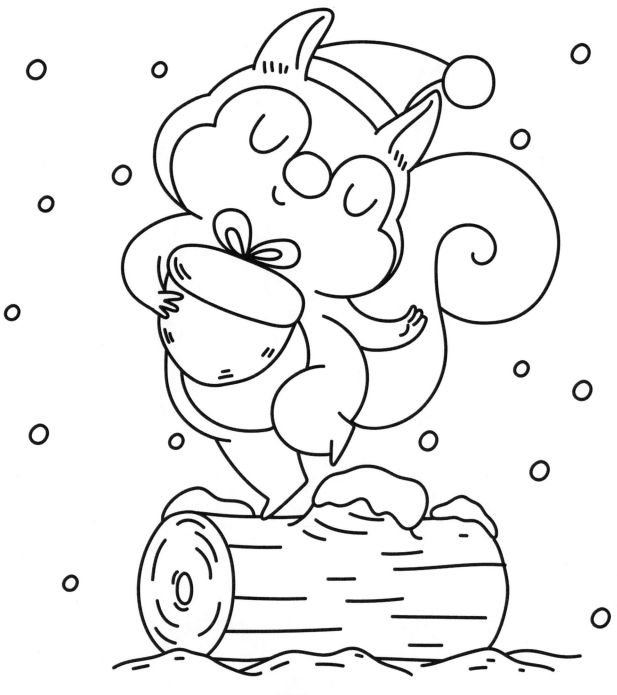

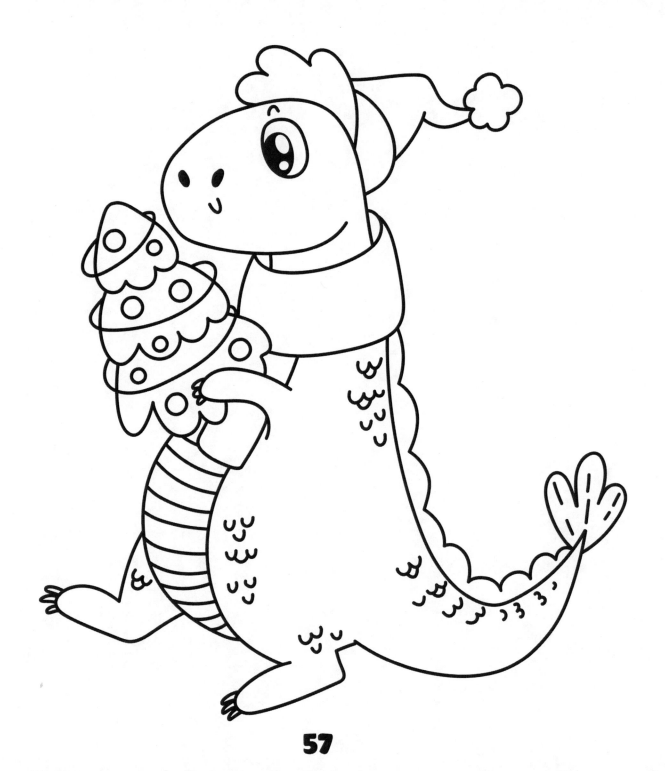

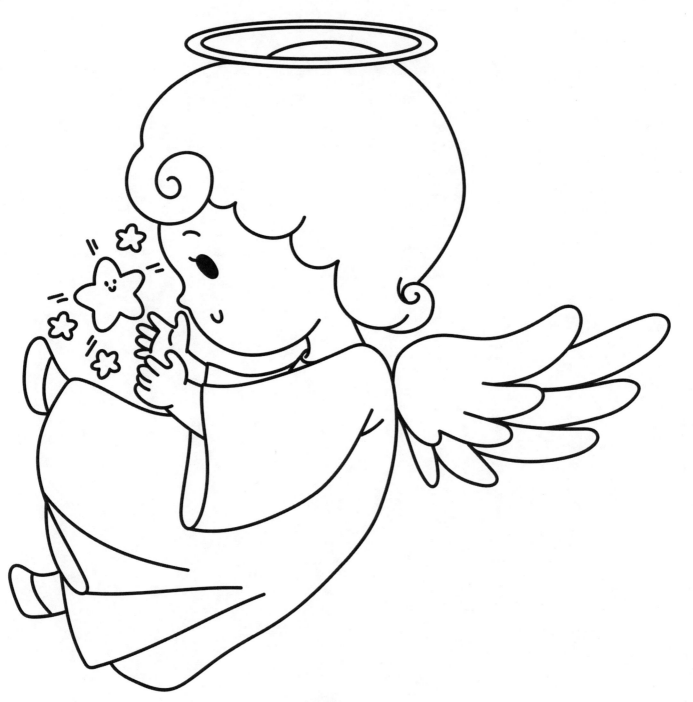

59

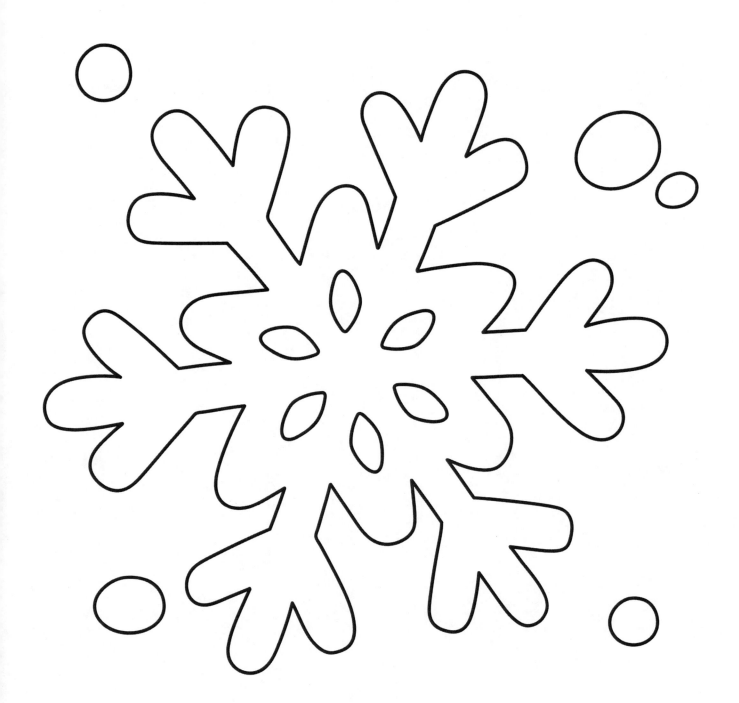

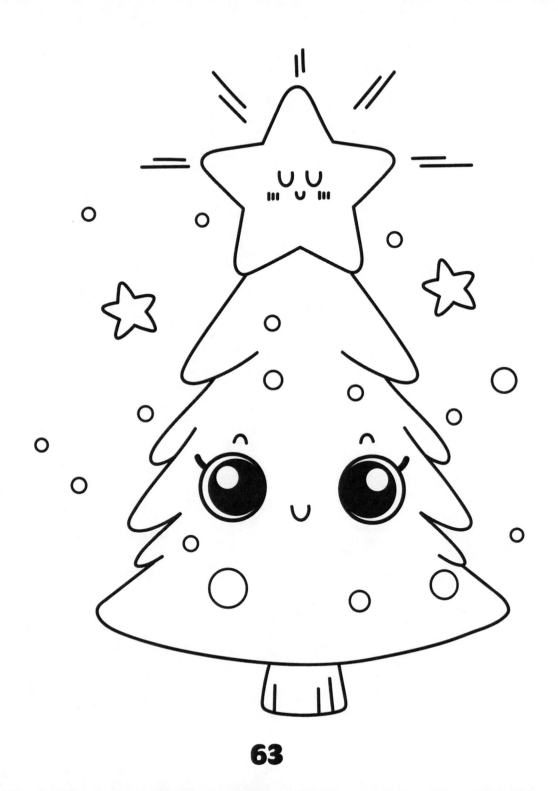

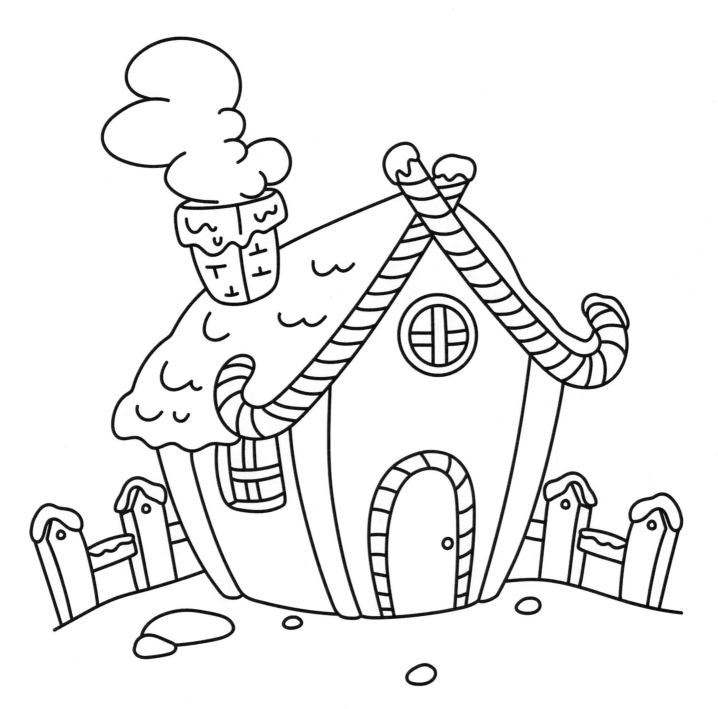

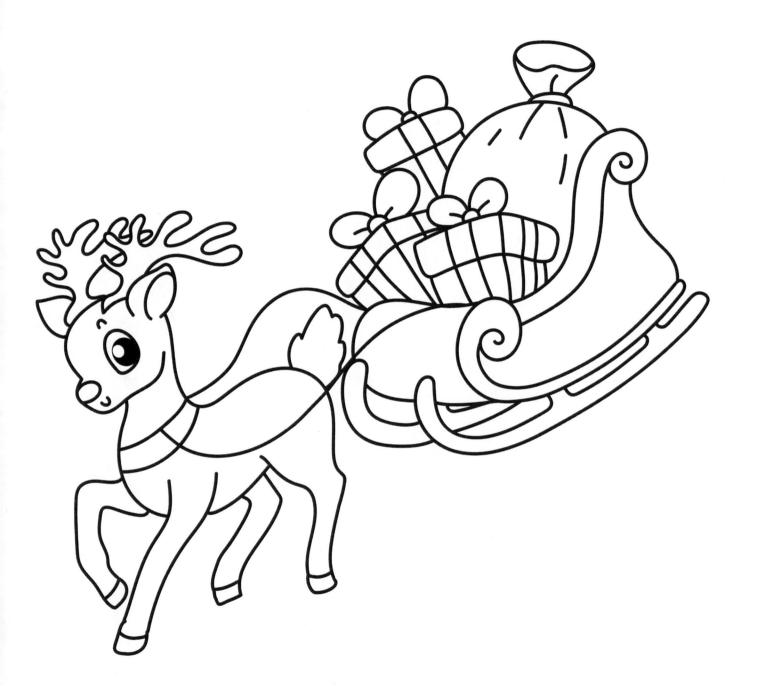

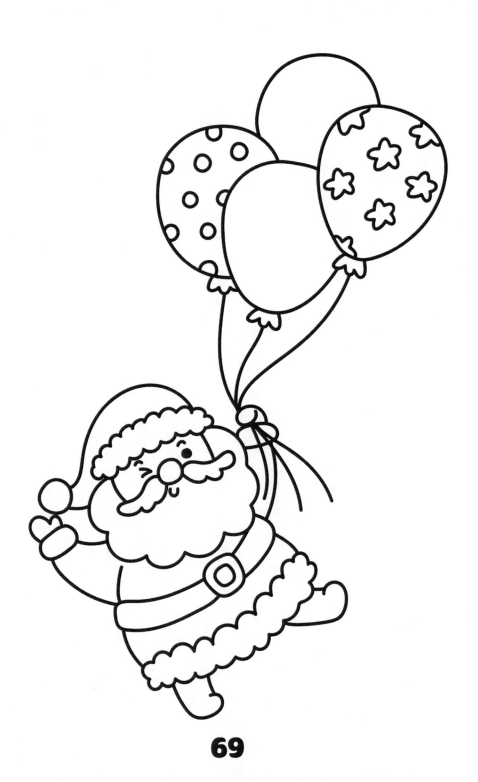

69

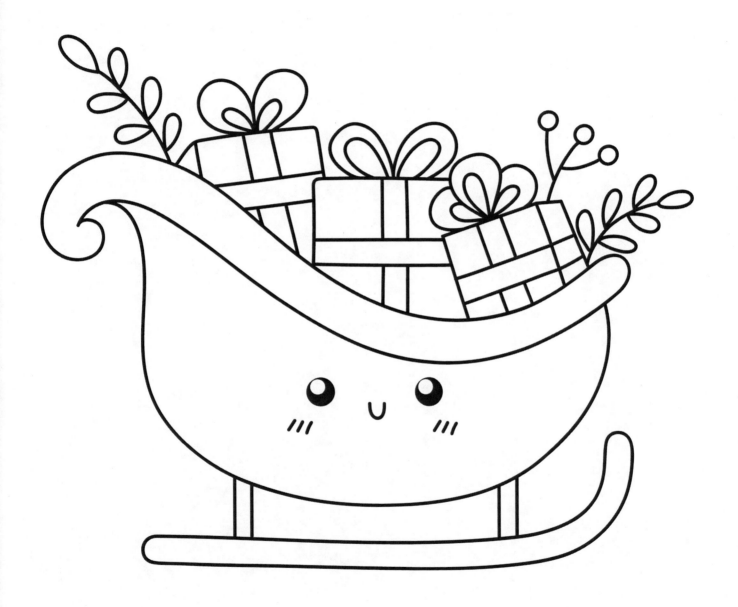

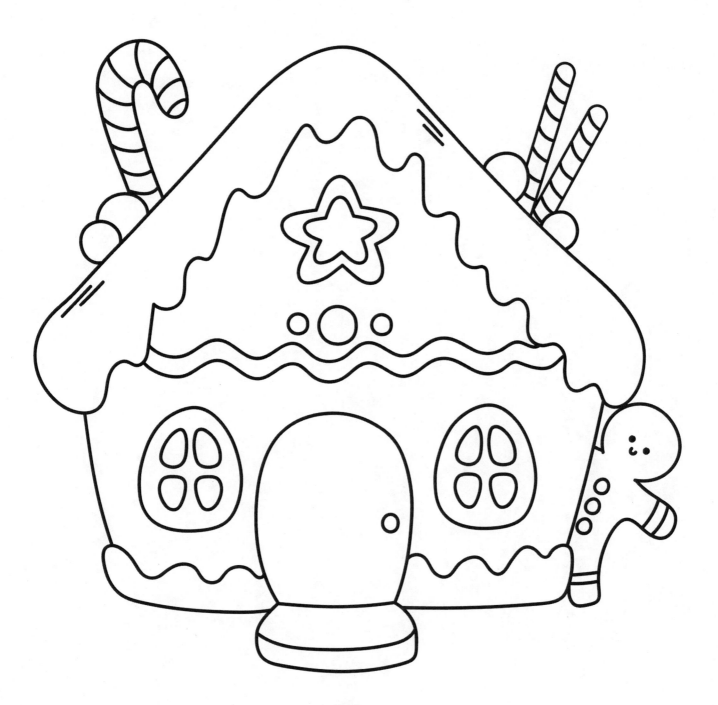

75

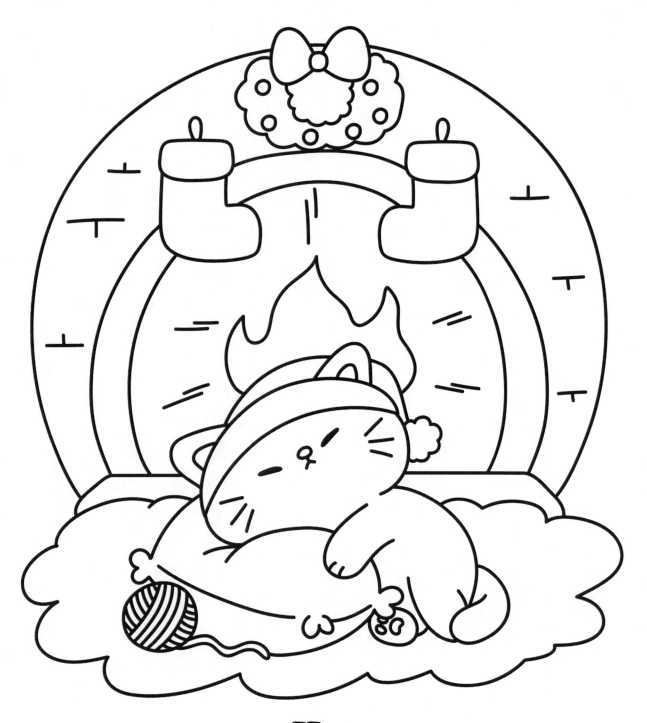

77

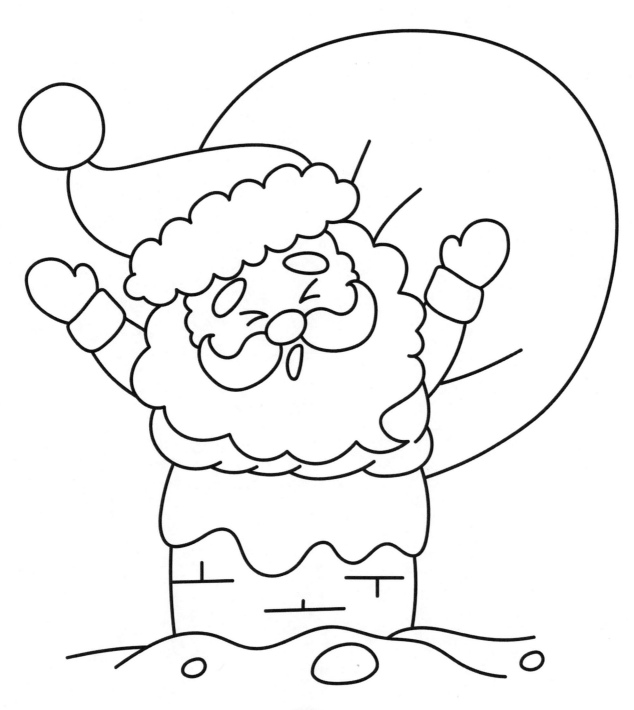

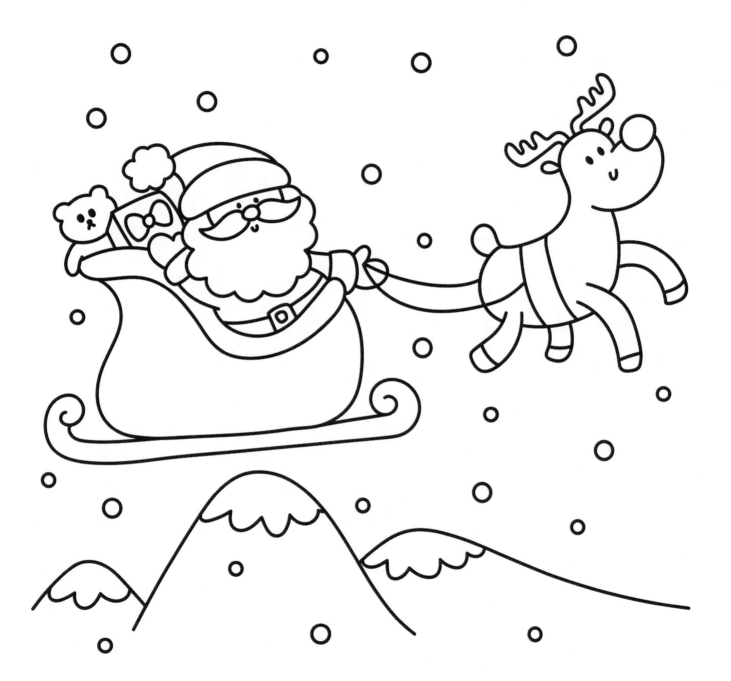

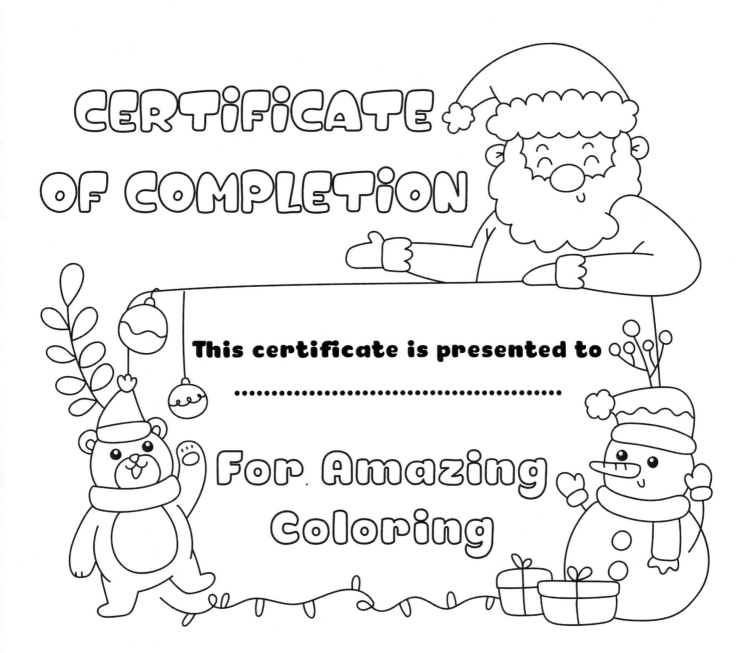

CERTIFICATE OF COMPLETION

This certificate is presented to

....

For Amazing Coloring

Made in United States
Cleveland, OH
09 December 2024

11578723R00046